Autism ABC

Written by:
Dr. Sherry L. Meinberg

Pictures by:
Rachael Mahaffey

ISBN: 1-4392-0205-2
ISBN-13: 9781439202050

Visit www.booksurge.com to order additional copies.

Autism ABC

Written by Dr. Sherry L. Meinberg
Pictures by Rachael Mahaffey

A is for autism. Sometimes things are easy for me to do and sometimes things are more difficult, because I have autism. And I am not alone.

Discuss the fact that two million people with autism are living in America, while many others remain undiagnosed. As it stands now, the CDC indicates that one out of every 150 children of about eight years old has this neurological disorder. The degree to which individuals are affected varies greatly, as each processes information in different ways. It generally shows up within the first three years of life, affecting both connection and communication, and is four to five times more common in boys. Autism is not a disease. Although no one knows what causes autism, there are plenty of theories and treatments. The recent rise in the statistics may be due to genetic, social, and environmental factors, or diets, or vaccines, or a combination thereof. In addition, there are now more thorough diagnoses for proper identification. Many older people will never be diagnosed. Granted, the autism experience creates many challenges to overcome, but also many gifts to treasure.

B is for bullies. Sometimes bullies bother me, because of the things they say and how they act. They don't know how to treat people, but I do.

Prevention is always better than intervention. Discuss safety, well-being, and how it feels to be teased. Know the difference between verbal and physical harassment, and how to respond. Children with autism, although gentle and sensitive, are often seen as outsiders. They provide easy marks for ridicule and abuse (name-calling, teasing, smirks, whispers, pushing, shoving, and tripping, with bursts of outright laughter and hostility), especially in the middle grades. Most school districts have a no-tolerance bullying policy, but teachers are often unaware of specific targeting, especially if it is not reported, because it is of short duration, even though it may be a daily occurrence. Keep a copy of the school policy for accountability purposes. Constant headaches and stomachaches may be signals that something is awry. Students may be afraid to complain about bullying, because specific threats may have been made. Check for bruises, scrapes, or scratches. Immediately inform the school of any problems. Never ignore bullying. Follow through.

C is for confused. Sometimes I get confused, because I don't always understand what people mean. But I am learning.

Often, those with autism don't follow directions because they are confused (too many words, said too quickly), so they don't know how to choose a proper response. Simplify your language. Give short, clear directions, such as, "Please shut the door," instead of long, involved sentences. Those with autism think logically and literally, and have trouble comprehending certain expressions. To avoid taking phrases literally, children must learn what they mean ("take a seat" means to sit down;"give me a hand" means to help me;

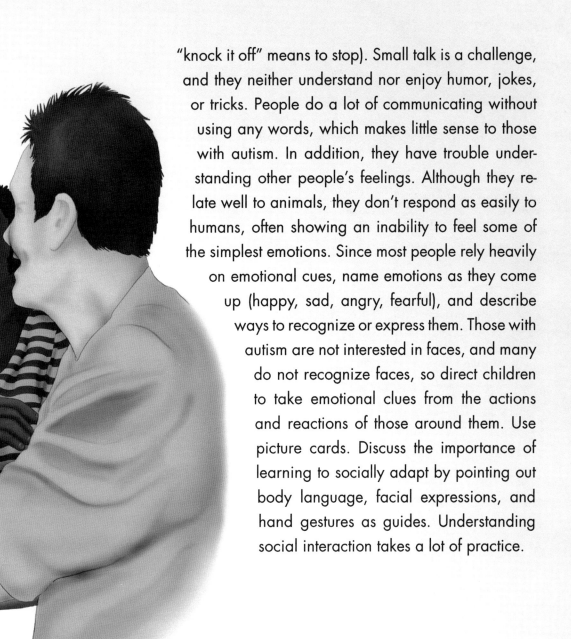

"knock it off" means to stop). Small talk is a challenge, and they neither understand nor enjoy humor, jokes, or tricks. People do a lot of communicating without using any words, which makes little sense to those with autism. In addition, they have trouble understanding other people's feelings. Although they relate well to animals, they don't respond as easily to humans, often showing an inability to feel some of the simplest emotions. Since most people rely heavily on emotional cues, name emotions as they come up (happy, sad, angry, fearful), and describe ways to recognize or express them. Those with autism are not interested in faces, and many do not recognize faces, so direct children to take emotional clues from the actions and reactions of those around them. Use picture cards. Discuss the importance of learning to socially adapt by pointing out body language, facial expressions, and hand gestures as guides. Understanding social interaction takes a lot of practice.

D is for different. Sometimes I feel different, but that's okay, because everyone is different in some way. We are all special.

Compare and contrast unique abilities. Rejoice in how much individuals have in common, and respect differences. Focus on things children with autism can do, rather than worry about the things they can't do. Encourage the understanding that people are all more alike than different.

E is for eyes. Sometimes I don't look at people's eyes when they talk, because I can hear them just fine. But everyone expects me to look into their eyes, so I will try my best.

Realize that you are not being ignored or treated rudely, if those with autism avoid eye contact. Direct eye contact can be irritating, and sometimes painful for them, and can result in a communication breakdown. Since visual input is so distracting, suggest positive strategies to aid in social interaction, such as: acknowledging someone by continuing to look at the ground, while giving quick sideways glances at the speaker; gradually facing the speaker and focusing on an earlobe or cheek; then looking closer to the eye area; later, gazing into the eyes for short periods; and finally, increasing the time spent looking directly in the eyes (some people actually count the seconds).

F is for friends. Sometimes I like to be around my friends, because it is fun just being together. We are happy to see each other.

Early on, there may be no sense at all of play as a mutual activity. Children with autism may appear to be self-absorbed, distant and detached, as they feel awkward and uncomfortable around others. Video games and computers are solo activities; friends require participation activities. Playing side-by-side with little interaction (swings, merry-go-rounds, and sandboxes provide good beginnings), or interacting with one another, or engaging in creative play, all offer a sense of connection and belonging. Those with autism often play with their toys in a different way. Encourage peers to mimic such play (lining up items, twirling toys, spinning wheels, and so forth), so that, at a later date, their own play may be mimicked. Discuss how to make and keep friends, recognizing that it is easier for them to respond to conversations than to initiate them. Urge peers to continue talking and playing, even if there is no response. Note that, at first, teens may find that being friendly on the phone or the computer may be easier than initiating actual face-to-face relationships. Understand that sharing is difficult for all children to learn, but especially for those with autism. Practice taking turns. Also, realize that friendship is a gradual process; it takes time to bond. Children must be taught how to show friendship. It appears that those with autism may be stronger than they realize (holding people and pets too tightly), and are sometimes seen by others to be too full of energy, or too rough and aggressive, in their play. Instead of allowing hitting to show affection, model hugging. Be persistent. Recognize that making friends, and sharing, both take time to learn, for everybody.

G is for good. Sometimes when I figure out something by myself, or when I learn something new, or when I do something right, I feel good, because I didn't give up. I am proud and happy.

Discuss accomplishments, and learning new things through practice, subtle changes, and reminders. Give kudos for effort. Look for things to praise. Catch them doing something right, and compliment them.

H is for honest. Sometimes I am too honest, because I am not careful with what I say. It makes others uncomfortable, so I will remember to watch what I say out loud.

We know that honesty is the best policy, but what one thinks about another person's appearance or actions is just an *opinion*. And that opinion may not be welcome. Although not purposefully impolite, a tactless, unintentional, or critical comment can be hurtful to others ("That mole on your nose is ugly!"; "You are so old, your face is wrinkled like a prune!"; "You are too fat."). Such remarks are irritating, intrusive, and annoying. Help them to consider the fact that even though something might actually be true, people may not want to hear about it. It's all right to think certain things, but it's not all right to say everything out loud. Discuss hurt feelings, embarrassment issues, and the inappropriateness of blurting out responses. Appropriate behavior must be learned, or the speaker will be thought of as rude.

I is for interests. Sometimes I will stare at something for a long time, because I find it so interesting. Not everyone shares my interests, because they have interests of their own.

Intense interests are considered to be positive. Discuss a fascination with certain items, or the intense preoccupation with particular subjects, often to the exclusion of other areas. At various times, there may be a compulsive collecting of different things (leaves, coins, marbles, books).Sometimes, children with autism will become so obsessed with a topic, that they will corner people with uninvited lectures. They will talk on and on and on about it, not allowing others to speak, or they may interrupt others in conversation, or simply talk over them. In their excitement and single-mindedness, they may be unaware that they are being impolite or rude. Yet, it is hard for them to sustain a conversation when the topic is of no interest to them. Often, they won't say anything, or will just walk away while the speaker is in midsentence. Tell them that this is a social mistake, and explain why they must be considerate of other people. Privately discuss the sharing, or give-and-take, of conversations. Watch TV discussions together. Practice turn-taking (playing cards, Chinese checkers, or board games may help in this regard). Teach social graces. Fixations can provide motivation for other subjects. Use and support those interests. Build on their strengths.

J is for jump. Sometimes I jump when I hear a loud noise or see a fast movement, because I am not expecting it. It is scary.

Discuss this startle effect as a safety response, explaining that it is a normal, acceptable reaction to an unforeseen event. Teach and drill safety rules. Often, it is the unexpectedness of the noise or the motion that affects them so much. For this reason, balloons—no matter how colorful—are often seen as potential explosions, along with birthday party horns and noisemakers; they do not represent a friendly, happy, carefree experience. (Note: Clowns, too—whether at parties, parades, or carnivals—also present a problem, with their grease-painted faces, exaggerated smiles, oversized shoes, garish colors, wild rainbow wigs, and unpredictable ways. And, since they often make balloon animals, they are doubly troublesome.)

K is for kind. Sometimes I meet people who are kind, nice, and polite. They pay attention to me, and make me feel good.

Discuss those people who are easy to like and comfortable to be around. Trade examples of others' kindnesses, as well as personal acts of kindness.

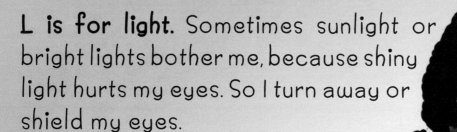

L is for light. Sometimes sunlight or bright lights bother me, because shiny light hurts my eyes. So I turn away or shield my eyes.

There is a strong reaction to bright lights. Discuss overly sensitive vision in the presence of fluorescent light, reflections, collision of colors, flashing lights, and so forth. Also discuss the sensation of seeing everything at once, or seeing too many details at the same time. Sunlight can cause eyes to become itchy and uncomfortable. When going outside on a sunny day, suggest wearing sunglasses or a ball cap with a large bill, as bright light can be physically painful to some, while others may not be able to see at all. At the very least, harsh lighting is annoying and distracting.

M is for movement. Sometimes I bounce, rock, spin, jump, clap, or flutter my hands, because it is soothing to me. Music, drumming, movement, and humming make me feel safe, comfortable, and in control.

If children are frightened or angry, it helps to calm themselves down with something that has a rhythm to it, such as tapping or drumming on almost any surface. Allow plenty of time for exercise or physical activities. The automatic movements used by children with autism are very effective for burning off energy. Teach them about the appropriate time and place to do so. Discuss various coping mechanisms.

N is for noise. Sometimes the noise is so loud, I cover my ears because it hurts. Too many different sounds make it hard to think, but I am getting used to it.

Discuss sensitive hearing and the noise factor. When children with autism are caught up in a swirl of people, it is hard for them to filter out background noise: too many people talking at once; different sounds competing at the same time, at the same volume; and distant sounds that interfere with closer sounds. Often, sounds are misinterpreted. Some sounds may appear scary (rain may sound like gunfire), while others cause physical pain. Noisy environments can be distracting and overwhelming, causing temper tantrums. Sometimes, they may hum or talk to themselves, to drown out excess noise. Warn of upcoming noise, so it will be expected (recess bells, fire drills, mixers, blenders, hairdryers, vacuums, and the like). Quiet breaks may be needed, when the noise level is too disturbing. Sound-protector earmuffs or earplugs may be worn, but if the sense of touch is too delicate, that they may hurt, as well. Consider using headphones. Try for a balance of busy and quiet, social and nonsocial activities.

O is for order. Sometimes I like to put things in a special order, or pattern, because placing them makes me feel good. I carefully arrange them by size, shape, or color.

Although arranging, classifying, and gazing rituals may show an aesthetic need for beauty and art, it may also be a way to control anxiety problems. The placement of pebbles, toys, shells, and the like, brings relief. And small items are manageable. Experts suggest that an arrangement marked by regularity, order, and balance, can represent a peaceful and beautiful world.

P is for parents. Sometimes my parents are sad, because I think and behave differently than they expect. We are still learning about each other, but we love each other just the same.

Discuss high expectations and different expectations; reinforce that children are loved and appreciated as is; and that every child has value and deserves respect.

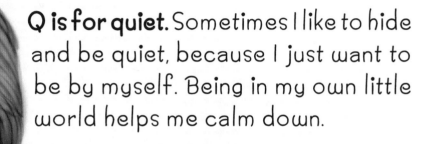

Q is for quiet. Sometimes I like to hide and be quiet, because I just want to be by myself. Being in my own little world helps me calm down.

There are times when those with autism need to retreat, to claim a sanctuary of sorts, or to draw inward, and curl up where the noisy and crowded world cannot interfere. Withdrawing under a bed, into a closet, or a favorite hidey-hole, shows that the child is over stimulated, and in need of calming experiences: alone, quiet, dark, snug, and warm. When overwhelmed, children may need or crave deep pressure, and will lie with a pillow, a sleeping bag, folded blankets, a heavy overcoat, couch cushions, or rugs on top of them, to get a sense of overall balance. Some will wear a padded, weighted vest. They need to feel safe, calm, secure, and comfortable. It is good that children are recognizing their limits, and taking care of themselves, as this self-imposed time-out is necessary for their mental health. To counteract the daily hustle and bustle and changing schedules in school, the quiet, order, space, and predictability of public libraries, museums, and art galleries may provide a sense of structure and contentment. Aquariums and zoos may also fill the need.

R is for repeat. Sometimes I repeat words, or questions, or do the same things, over and over again, because I like things to be the same. It makes me feel calm and in control.

Instead of answering you, some children with autism may simply repeat verbatim what you've just said ("What are you doing?", "What are you doing?"). Or they may sing commercial jingles over and over, driving everyone to the brink. Recognize that this may be a way to release pressure, and pacify issues of nervousness or anxiety. Discuss what it is about certain favorite words that they find intriguing, to understand why they are endlessly repeated. Know that the need for repetition also extends to favorite activities, special routes, and attachment to specific places.

S is for surprise. Sometimes I don't like surprises, because I want to know exactly what is going to happen next. Even when I am uncomfortable with changes in my day, I try my best to deal with them in a good way.

Contrast routines, rituals, and daily schedules, with out-of-the-blue unexpected changes, and surprises that weren't appreciated. Provide scheduled, structured activities at home. Try to serve meals at the same time, and maintain the same bath time and bedtime hour, with a predictable pattern (such as: undress, bath, pajamas, brush teeth, in bed, story, tucked in, prayer, kiss, lights off, sleep). To counteract nervousness or frustration, explain in advance when a change is going to   happen. Give reminders. A posted daily schedule, in pictures or words, can provide security. Cross off the activities as they are accomplished. Or move picture cards around, to show that a particular activity will be experienced later in the day. A posted weekly calendar (for special events, vacations, and such), on which you cross off the days, communicates when a change is going to take place, and provides comfort.

T is for touch. Sometimes I don't want people to touch me, hug me, kiss me, tickle me, or even shake my hand, because it hurts my skin. It feels like they are poking me, or pinching me, or giving me a shot. I like to feel comfortable.

Any unexpected touch is uncomfortable. At school, simply sitting on a rug with other students, or standing in a line, may be difficult for those with autism, due to the fear that someone may touch them. Placing them in the back row on the rug, or in back of the line may be helpful (ask first). Placing their desks in the back row allows them to look over the students, while not having to make any eye contact with them, causing them to be more relaxed and content. It also allows them to pace,without bothering other students. When excused for recess, lunch, or to go home, they may hang back, waiting for others to leave first, afraid of being pushed or jostled. They may be anxious or afraid in the hallways. Understand that their time in school may be based on avoiding situations in which they may be touched. They may prefer to sit at a table in a corner, or against the wall, so others won't surround them. Understand that when you give a supportive squeeze to a shoulder, or a pat on the head, or ruffle their hair, it can be distressing to them, sending the wrong message entirely. Brushing teeth, shampooing hair, and shaving can also hurt. Discuss sensitivity to textures (tags or stitching on clothes, scratchy materials). Dress children in soft clothing. Know that some tactile sensations can act as a kind of comforter. Recognize, too, that the sense of touch also affects eating habits, as some foods are painful to eat. Many foods are experienced as too prickly, too slimy, or too hot or cold, which greatly limits the number of foods eaten. Because of their high sensitivity in all senses, many are unable to tolerate the texture, offensive smell, vivid color, strong taste, or sound (crunchy) of food. Add that to severe allergies—which are linked to autism spectrum disorders—and some children have a bland diet of less than ten foods. Others may not eat for several days. As a result, children with autism have become known as finicky or picky eaters.

U is for upset. Sometimes I get upset when things aren't in their usual place, because I like things to be neat and tidy. I don't like messy or dirty or cluttered places, so I put things away as best I can.

There is often an obsessive need for order. Those with autism like things to be done in a certain way, and in a certain order. Changes in the environment are not welcome. Many will know immediately if something in their rooms has been moved. When something is out of place, or when a room is too cluttered, it can feel unsettling and overwhelming.

V is for video. Sometimes I watch videos, because I like to see cartoons, and movies, and even TV commercials. I get excited about them, and learn lots of new things.

Discuss words, catch phrases, and lines of dialogue, taken from the repeated viewing of videos, which can be echoed to gain confidence in language usage. Focus and practice. Emotional emphasis, body language, and gestures, can be mimicked, as well, in social situations.

W is for words. Sometimes I don't know what words to say, because what I'm thinking is too hard to explain. When I get stuck, I get frustrated, but I am learning more about words every day.

When children with autism can't find the proper words to express themselves, they may mumble to themselves, talk gibberish, use sign language, or just walk away. They think and listen in a very logical and literal way, which often makes communication difficult. Discuss idioms, and slang expressions, which are so different from exact meanings. Use simple, clear language. Experts suggest that just saying, "Wow!" with an accompanying smile, can be an acceptable response to almost anything.

X is for extra. Sometimes I need extra help, because I want to get things right. I find an adult or a friend to show me what to do.

Discuss and model how to ask for assistance. Practice.

Y is for yell. Sometimes I yell, and scream, and holler, because too much is happening all around me. I get all mixed up and frustrated, but I am working on controlling myself.

Sensory overload is common. Being overwhelmed by too many sights, sounds, smells, and people, all at once, can cause considerable distress and bewilderment to those with autism. New situations can cause them to be anxious and uncomfortable. Discuss outbursts, anger issues, and tantrums. Experts remind us that all behavior is communication; that physical actions—biting, head banging, and such—are all forms of communication for those who don't have effective skills to relay their message (those who are ignored, utilize little oral speech, or have no communication devices). Teach children to behave appropriately. Use the phrase, "The rule is . . ." Then explain why the rule exists. Make sure that discipline between home and school is uniform, and that there are consequences for bad behavior. Be firm, but fair. Make sure that the rules are always the same, and the response is always the same. Be consistent.

Z is for zoo. Sometimes I feel like an animal in the zoo, because I think everyone is staring at me. But I look at them, too.

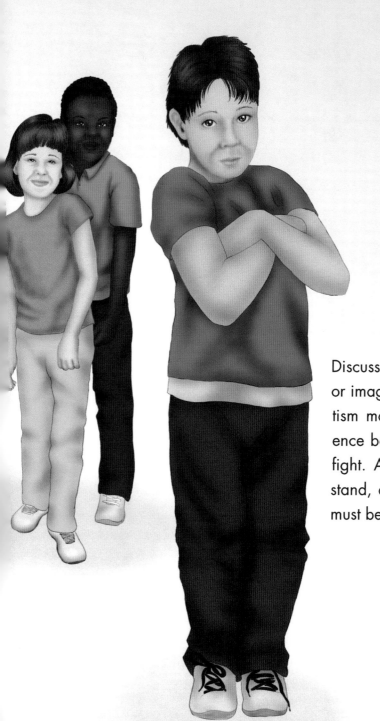

Discuss and encourage play-acting. Pretending or imagining may be difficult, as some with autism may not be able to recognize the difference between a make-believe fight and a real fight. Abstract concepts are difficult to understand, as are emotions and empathy. Feelings must be taught.

I have autism, and I am not alone. Many, many people have autism. It is a way of being. We have special skills and special challenges, just like everyone else. And we can all be happy. Together, we can make our world more beautiful.

2623411

Made in the USA